Fossil Ridge Public Library District
386 Kennedy Road
Braidwood, Illinois 60408

8/99

The Conflict Resolution Library™

Dealing with Stealing

• Lisa K. Adams •

The Rosen Publishing Group's
PowerKids Press™
New York

Published in 1997 by The Rosen Publishing Group, Inc.
29 East 21st Street, New York, NY 10010

First Edition

Book Design: Erin McKenna

Photo Credits: Cover by Ira Fox; p. 4 © D. Hall/Camerique/H. Armstrong Roberts, Inc.; pp. 7, 12 © Camerique/H. Armstrong Roberts, Inc.; p. 8 © Blumebild/H. Armstrong Roberts, Inc.; p. 11 © H. Armstrong Roberts, Inc.; p. 15 © S. Feld/H. Armstrong Roberts, Inc.; p. 16 © Dusty Willison/International Stock Photo; p. 19 by Seth Dinnerman; p. 20 © L. Powers/H. Armstrong Roberts, Inc.

Adams, Lisa K.
    Dealing with stealing / by Lisa K. Adams.
       p.   cm. — (The conflict resolution library)
    Includes index.
    Summary: Explains what stealing is, why it is wrong, the difference between stealing and sharing, and the consequences of theft.
    ISBN 0-8239-5072-7
    1. Stealing—Juvenile literature. [1. Stealing.] I. Title. II. Series.
HQ784.S65A33 1997
364.16'2—dc21
                                                         97-4147
                                                          CIP
                                                           AC

Manufactured in the United States of America

Contents

1	Stealing Is Always Wrong	5
2	Ownership	6
3	Sharing	9
4	Why Do People Steal?	10
5	It's Never Worth It	13
6	Trust	14
7	Stealing Isn't Cool	17
8	Bobby and Darren	18
9	What to Do If You Steal	21
10	Be Proud of Yourself	22
	Glossary	23
	Index	24

Stealing Is Always Wrong

Have you ever taken something that doesn't belong to you and not given it back? If you have, then that's stealing. It doesn't matter if the stolen object is money or a pack of gum, it's still stealing.

Have you ever had something stolen from you, such as your bike or a favorite toy? It can make you feel terrible. Stealing hurts the person you steal from. But it hurts the person who steals too.

◀ If you take something that doesn't belong to you, you're hurting yourself as well as the person you've stolen from.

5

Ownership

When you were very young, you probably didn't understand the idea of **ownership** (OH-ner-ship). If you saw something that you wanted, you took it.

Now that you're older, you understand that certain things don't belong to you. You know that if you want something, you either have to ask the owner if you can **borrow** (BAR-oh) it, or you have to buy it. You can't just take it.

Most young kids don't understand that some things don't ▶ belong to them. They may get upset when they can't just take something when they want it.

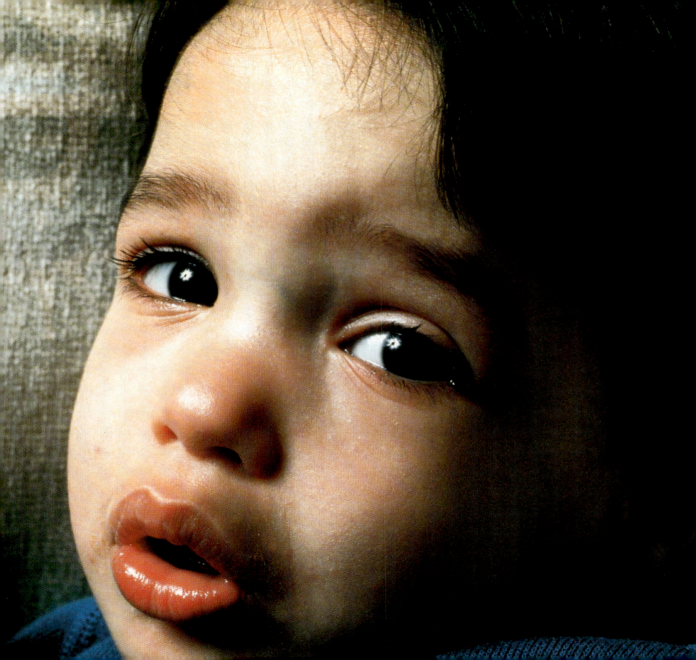

Sharing

If you are at a friend's house and she has a toy that you want to play with, don't just take it. Ask her if you can borrow it for a little while. This means that she lets you have it for a short time, and then you give it back to her.

What if your friend says no, that she doesn't want to share? Then you have to **accept** (ak-SEPT) that. But a good friend will see that sharing is best for everybody.

◀ Sharing can make you feel good about yourself and about being with your friends.

Why Do People Steal?

Some people steal because they want something that they don't or can't have. Others think that stealing is exciting.

Lots of kids steal. Kids who have money steal just as much as kids who don't. Some don't realize that it's wrong. Some just can't resist the **temptation** (tem-TAY-shun). Just because a person has stolen something does not mean he or she is a bad person. It just means that he or she has made a bad **decision** (dih-SIH-zhun).

Kids might think stealing is an easy way to get something that they want. ▶

It's Never Worth It

Tanya went to the store with her mom. She really wanted a pack of gum, but she knew her mom wouldn't buy it for her. So she stole it when she thought no one was watching.

The clerk saw her take the gum and told her to give it back. Tanya knew that stealing was wrong. Tanya's mom was very **disappointed** (dis-uh-POYN-ted) in her. Tanya never knew how bad stealing would make her feel. She felt **guilty** (GIL-tee). She decided never to steal again.

◀ Stealing can make you feel bad about yourself.

13

Trust

Stealing can **damage** (DAM-ij) the trust that people have in you. If you steal something, your friends and family may find it hard to trust that you will not do it again.

If you steal something, don't lie about it. Be honest and explain why you did it. Return what you stole and promise not to do it anymore. In time, you will earn people's trust again. They will see that you are able to keep your promise not to steal.

14

Stealing can make someone feel like he or she can't trust you. ▶

Stealing Isn't Cool

You may have a friend who will ask you to steal with her. She might dare you to do it or tell you that it's cool to steal. Don't let her **persuade** (per-SWAYD) you to steal. Tell her you don't steal and you aren't going to start.

Think about this friend who wants you to steal. Do you really want to be friends with a person who steals? What would stop her from stealing *your* things? You can avoid trouble by having friends who don't steal.

◀ Having friends who don't steal is a good choice.

Bobby and Darren

Bobby and Darren went to the store for Bobby's mother. Darren dared Bobby to steal something with him. Bobby wanted his friend to think he was cool. So they stole some candy. Bobby didn't get caught. But Darren did. The store owner called the boys' parents. Bobby's parents said they were proud of him for not stealing. But Bobby wasn't proud of himself. He felt guilty and **ashamed** (uh-SHAYMD) of what he did. Bobby knew he had done the wrong thing by stealing.

Stealing can make you feel bad. But not admitting that you stole something will make you feel worse. ▶

What to Do If You Steal

If you have stolen something and you want to do the right thing, the first thing to do is return what you stole. If you took a candy bar, tell your parents and have them take you back to the store. Return the candy bar and **apologize** (uh-POL-uh-jyz) to the store owner. This won't be easy. It's embarrassing to admit that you have stolen something. But chances are, your parents will be proud of you for being brave and setting things straight.

◀ Telling the truth is the best choice you can make—for yourself and for others.

Be Proud of Yourself

If you see a new toy or game that you really want, think of ways other than stealing to make it yours. Ask your parents if you can earn money by doing extra chores around the house to help pay for it. Working for something is much more **rewarding** (re-WARD-ing) than stealing. If you don't steal, you won't feel guilty. You won't feel ashamed. Instead, you will feel proud that you worked hard and earned what you wanted!

Glossary

accept (ak-SEPT) To recognize something as the way it is.

apologize (uh-POL-uh-jyz) To say you're sorry.

ashamed (uh-SHAYMD) Feeling bad or uncomfortable about yourself.

borrow (BAR-oh) To get something from another person with the understanding that it will be returned.

damage (DAM-ij) To harm something.

decision (dih-SIH-zhun) To make up your mind about something.

disappointed (dis-uh-POYN-ted) To feel let down.

guilty (GIL-tee) How someone feels after doing something he or she knows is wrong.

ownership (OH-ner-ship) The idea that certain things belong to certain people.

persuade (per-SWAYD) To convince someone to do something for you.

rewarding (re-WARD-ing) Something that makes you feel good after you do it.

temptation (tem-TAY-shun) An urge to do something.

Index

A
acceptance, 9
apologizing, 21
ashamed, feeling,
18

B
borrowing, 6, 9

D
decision, 10
disappointment,
13

G
guilty, feeling, 13,
22

L
lie, telling a, 14

O
ownership, 6

P
persuading others
to steal, 17
promising not to
steal, 14
proud, being, 21,
22

R
rewarding, 22

S
sharing, 9

T
temptation, 10,
trust, 14
damaging, 14

24